HUMAN RESOURCE COLORING BOOK

This Book Belongs To:

____

____

COLOR TEST PAGE

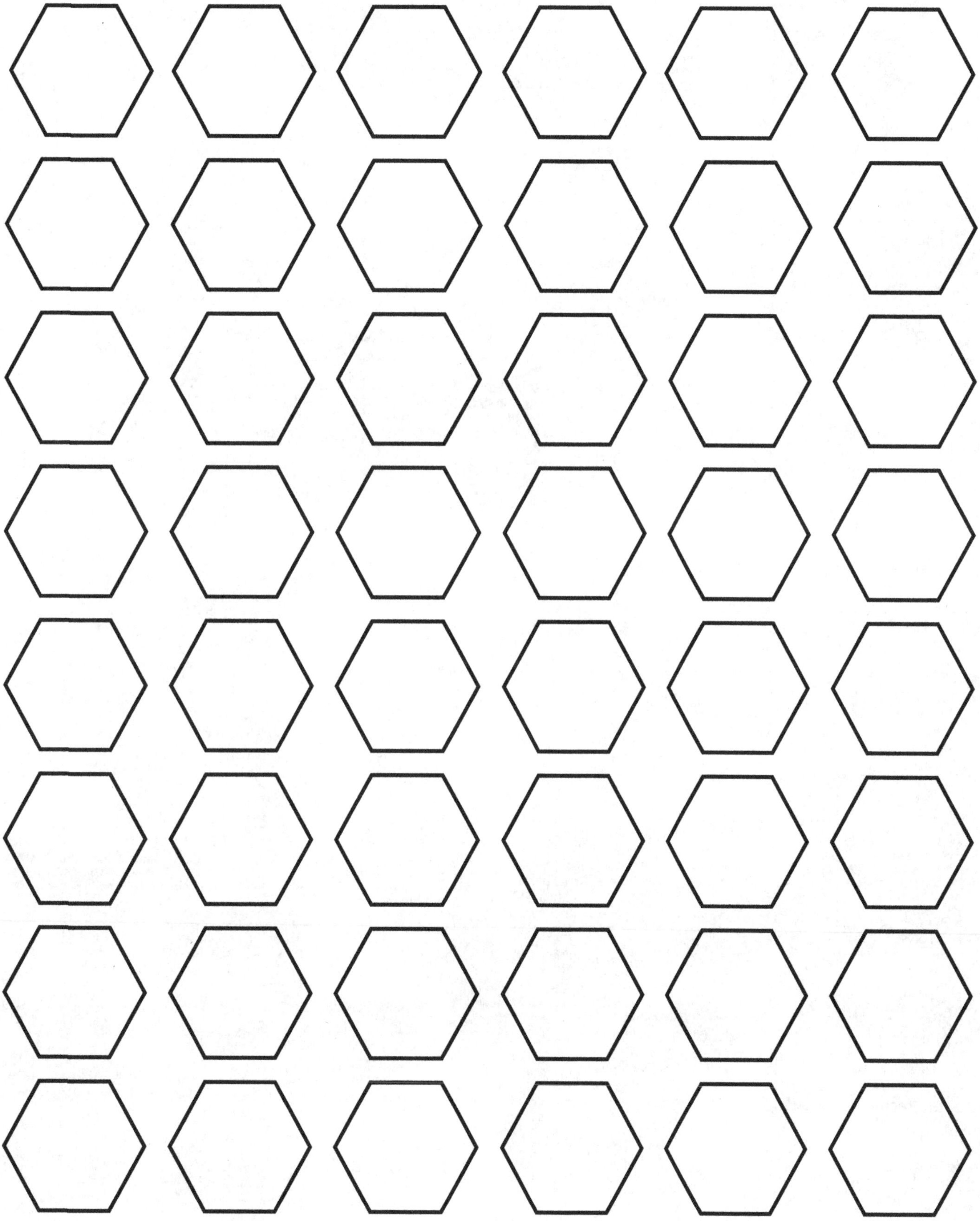

HR LIFE
I make it
LOOK EASY

IF IT'S NOT
DOCUMENTED
IT NEVER
HAPPENED

I'M AN
HR
PROFESSIONAL
IT'S MY
JOB
TO JUDGE YOU

YOU CAN'T SPELL
HERO
WITHOUT HR

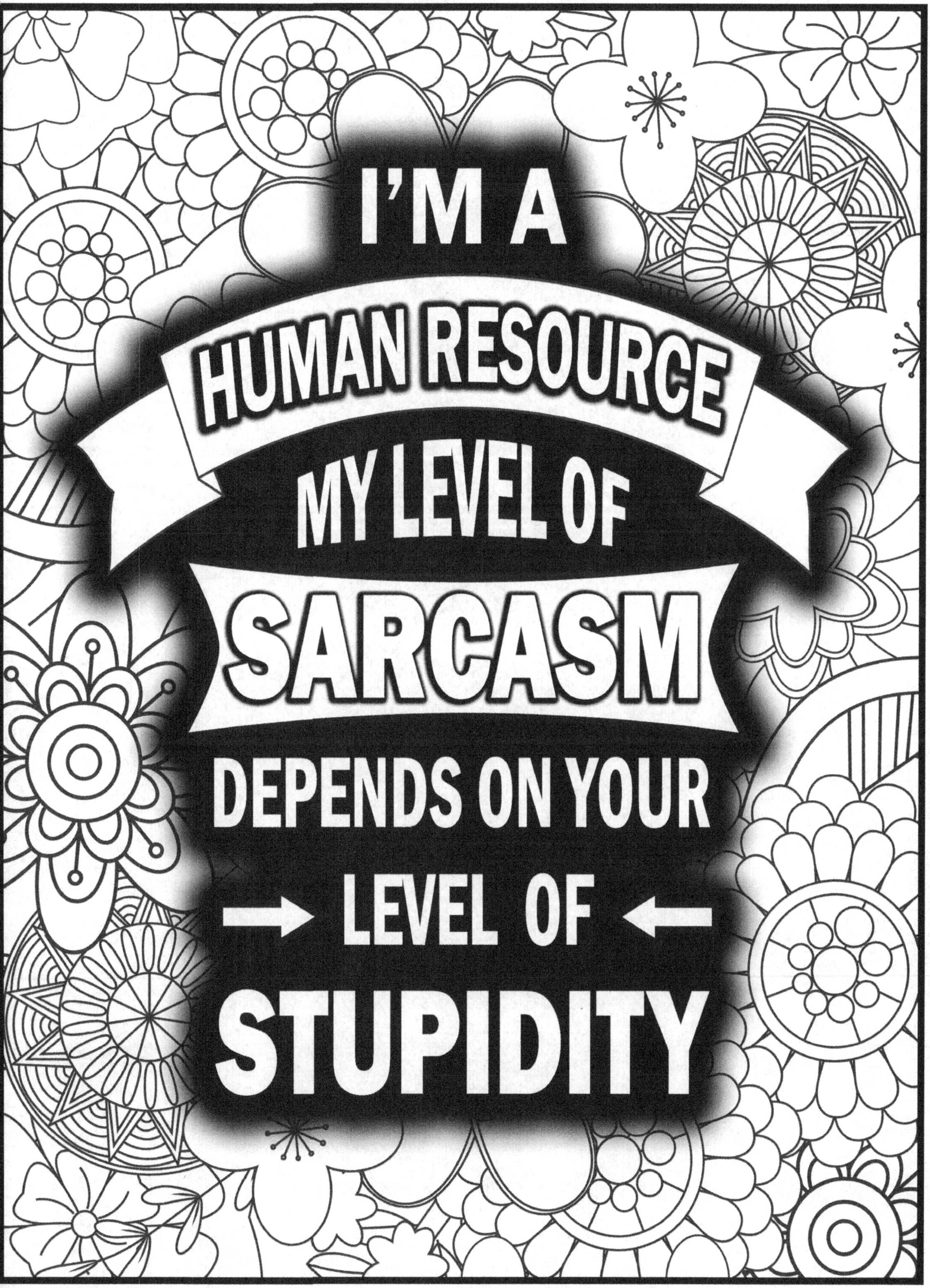
I'M A
HUMAN RESOURCE
MY LEVEL OF
SARCASM
DEPENDS ON YOUR
LEVEL OF
STUPIDITY

THIS
HR
IS A
freaking
LEGEND

WHAT HAPPENS
IN HR
STAYS
IN HR

I Used To Have
A LIFE
But I Decided
TO BE AN
HR

HR
WE PUT THE
FUN IN
DYSFUNCTIONAL
TEAM

PART-TIME
HUMAN RESOURCE
Professional
FULL-TIME
HUMAN

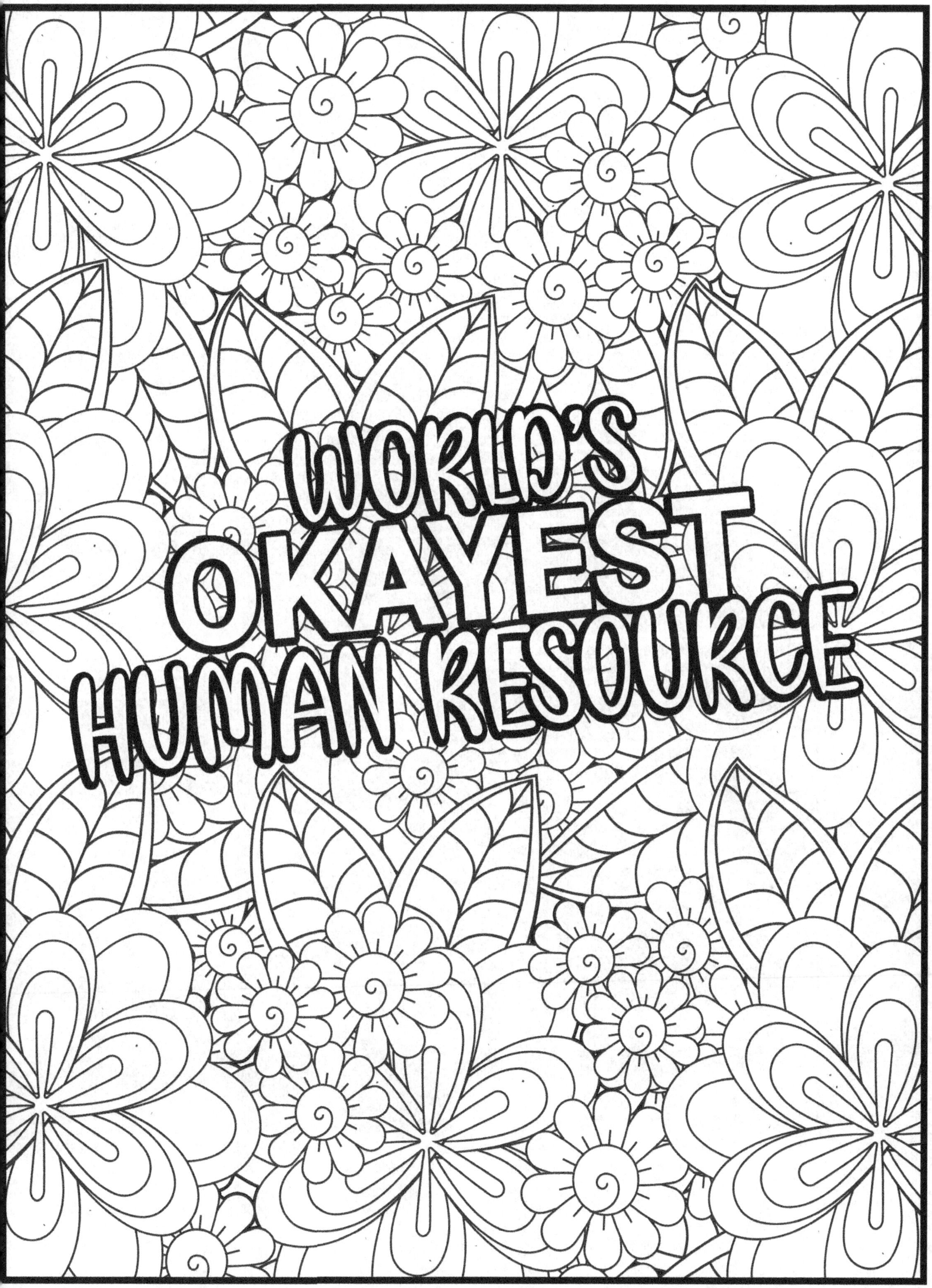
WORLD'S
OKAYEST
HUMAN RESOURCE

HR LLAMA
AIN'T GOT TIME
FOR YOUR
DRAMA

I'M IN
HR
I Can't Fix
CRAZY
BUT I CAN
DOCUMENT IT

BEING A
HUMAN RESOURCE
IS EASY,IT'S LIKE
RIDING A BIKE
EXCEPT THE BIKE
IS ON FIRE
YOU'RE ON FIRE
EVERYTHING IS ON FIRE

No Matter
HOW HARD
Life Gets
AT LEAST YOU ARE AN
HR

I AM
SILENTLY
JUDGING
YOUR CV

I LIKE TO PARTY
AND BY
PARTY
I MEAN DO
PAYROLL
WITHOUT ANY
INTERRUPTIONS

I'M AN
HR
Don't Ask Me
WHAT I'M
DOING

DON'T MAKE ME
USE MY
HUMAN
RESOURCE
VOICE

I'M NOT
ARGUING
I'M JUST
EXPLAINING
WHY I'M
RIGHT

THIS
HR
IS OFF
DUTY

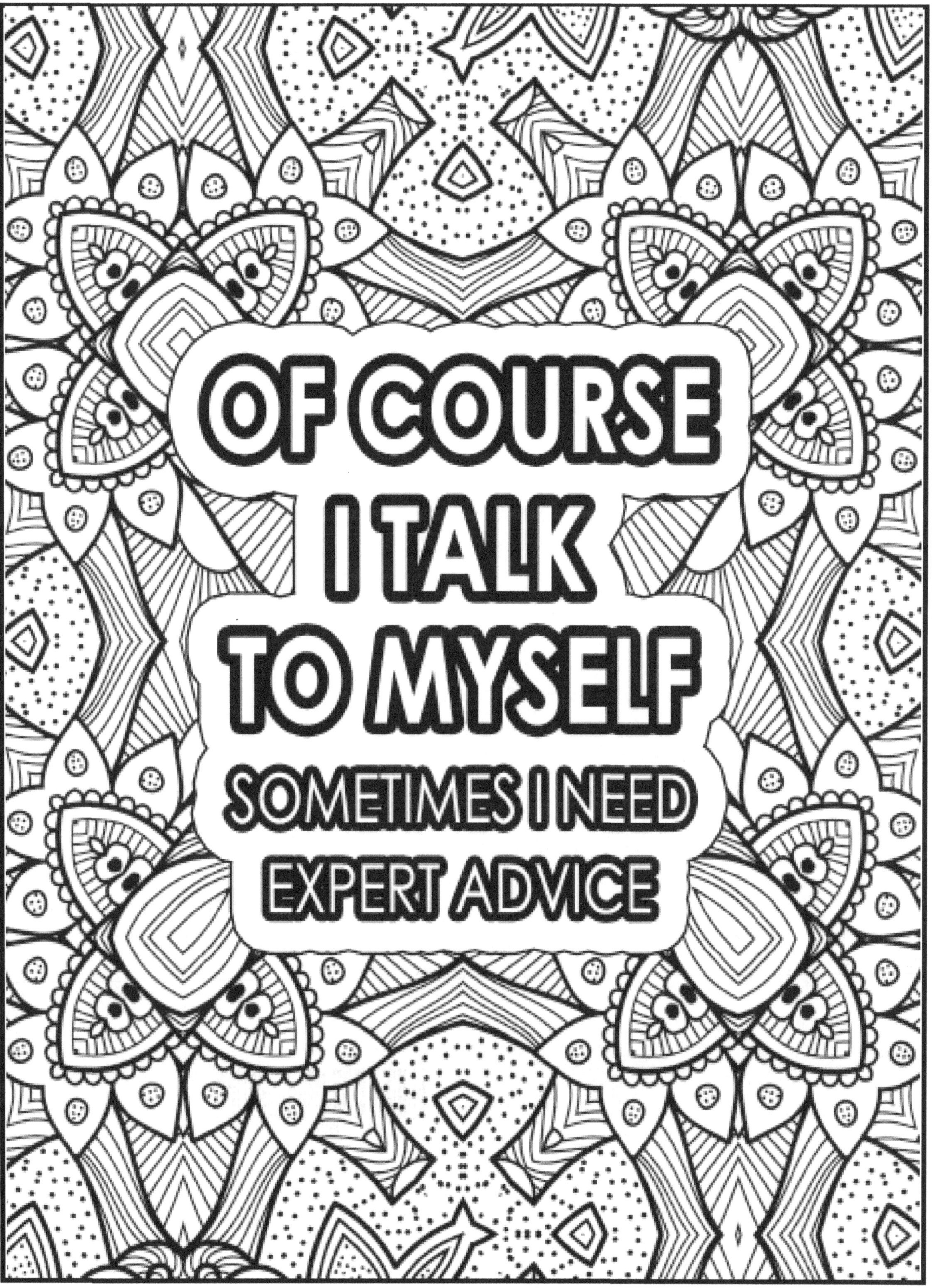
OF COURSE
I TALK
TO MYSELF
SOMETIMES I NEED
EXPERT ADVICE

Made in the USA
Las Vegas, NV
12 December 2024

13950697R00026